Teaching During the Pandemic

By: Dawn Sessom

Published by She Rises Studios Publishing www.SheRisesStudios.com.

ISBN: 978-1-968061-33-3

Table of Contents

Introduction

McKinsey & Company (2021) reported that by the end of the 2020–2021 school year, students were on average five months behind in math and four months behind in reading. Students in high-poverty schools were hit hardest, with some falling up to 12 months behind. The Northwest Evaluation Association (NWEA) found that as of 2022, many students were still 1 to 2 grade levels behind in core subjects. Early elementary grades (K–2), where foundational reading and math skills are developed, were most affected. Many children missed crucial classroom time for phonics, handwriting, number sense, and social-emotional development. Some kindergartners and first graders enter 2nd or even 3rd grade without ever having had a full year of in-person learning.

Teaching During the Pandemic captures the roller coaster of emotions, challenges, and breakthroughs that teachers, students, and parents experienced during one of the most disruptive times in modern education. This book takes readers behind the screens into the virtual classrooms where educators had to quickly adapt, students struggled to stay engaged, and parents juggled new roles in a rapidly changing learning environment. As the world navigated uncharted territory, teaching transformed overnight. Through firsthand accounts and reflective insights, this book sheds light on the resilience, creativity, and determination it took to keep learning alive—even when the classroom doors were closed.

Being a teacher for over twenty years, I never imagined I would one day find myself teaching students through a computer screen. The transition from one-on-one, in-person instruction to guiding students with little to no technological skills was overwhelming and, at times, disheartening. As an educator, I've had the privilege of working in a variety of school settings, serving students from diverse racial, cultural, and educational backgrounds. I once considered myself a seasoned expert in the classroom—but nothing could have prepared me for the unprecedented challenges that came with pandemic teaching. It forced me to relearn, adapt, and stretch in ways I never thought possible.

The purpose of writing this book is not only to enlighten readers about the realities we faced during the pandemic, but also to shift the narrative around what education looks like today. The truth is, we will never be the same—but that doesn't mean we can't be better. The pandemic exposed the vulnerabilities in our educational system, but it also opened the door to innovation. Education was thrust into a new world—one that now demands students, teachers, and schools adapt to the fast-paced, ever-evolving demands of 21st-century life. This book is a call to reflection, growth, and ultimately transformation.

In my book, you will get a deep dive into the real experiences, challenges, and triumphs that educators, students, and families encountered during one of the most defining moments in modern education. You'll explore the following themes:

- **The Sudden Shift** – How classrooms across the world transitioned overnight from face-to-face learning to virtual instruction.
- **Digital Disparities** – The technological divide that left many students behind and exposed deep inequities in access and resources.
- **The Emotional Toll** – The impact on mental health for students, teachers, and parents navigating isolation, uncertainty, and burnout.
- **Reinventing Teaching** – Creative strategies teachers used to engage learners, build community, and maintain academic rigor online.
- **Parent Partnerships** – How family involvement took on new meaning as learning entered the home.
- **Lessons for the Future** – Reflections on what we must carry forward to build a more inclusive, innovative, and resilient education system.

Overall, I encourage my readers to enjoy this book because it is a heartfelt journey through one of the most challenging yet transformative periods in education. It is a tribute to the resilience of teachers, the adaptability of students, and the strength of families who pushed through the unknown together. This book is not just about what went wrong, it's about what we learned, how we grew, and how we can reimagine education for a better future. Whether you're an educator, parent, or simply someone who values learning, I hope this book inspires you to see the possibilities that can emerge even in the most uncertain times.

CHAPTER ONE

THE DAY MY LIFE CHANGED AND MY CAREER TOO!

3/13/2020

So, it all started in December; I was fortunate to have the opportunity to secure employment with the DeKalb County School District. I had just finished student teaching and obtained my certification by completing the edTPA, which was the most rigorous process of my life. This portfolio felt like a dissertation in its entirety, as it was required to become certified. It was utterly insane, and I must say it was the start of my diagnosis of anxiety.

I was grateful to gain a position as a first-grade teacher. When I entered the classroom, I had to change the class environment and the students significantly. This class has had a constant rotation of substitute teachers since October. This was a task within itself because this class truly loved their first-grade teacher, who left to take on another position. Here, I battled all types of emotions with my students. Yes, I had teaching experience, but I never started a school term in the middle of the first quarter. This was a new experience. My focus was getting to know my students and creating an environment that helps them open and express their feelings and themselves. I also believed in morning meetings where we sat and talked for over 15 minutes about our feelings and emotions. This was the primary reason my students didn't take long to adjust. By December, my students and I had finally settled into the groove of class expectations. I built a relationship with my students' parents and was preparing for the spring semester, along with all the great activities I had planned.

MARCH 13, 2020!!!!!!

BREAKING NEWS!!! A new virus that was currently incurable and causing so many to become sick has now caused a PANDEMIC across our Country. Governors must take immediate action, and schools MUST CLOSE!!! We are asking everyone to quarantine until further notice! Only essential workers with badges are permitted to work currently.

I wake up to this?!?! What? Are you serious? I noticed that my students were frequently absent from school due to fevers, coughs, stomachaches, diarrhea, and congestion. As a teacher, this is a common occurrence. We see this all the time. But now schools all over the country are CLOSED! I read my emails; my principal calls for a mandatory meeting in the cafeteria at 8:30 a.m. Upon arrival, I was greeted with hand sanitizer and a mask. We must wear a mask. What? This is crazy! I was also told I could not touch anyone, and we had to be six feet apart.

We went into the cafeteria. I look around, and all I see are my coworkers sitting too far apart, wearing gloves, masks, and nursing outfits, with sanitizers and Lysol nearby. I no longer noticed anyone anymore. My principal got on the mic and said, "This has been a crazy school year!" I had to agree! Along with this being my first year at Idlewood, it was also my principal's first year in GA, as a principal and at Idlewood. She says, "We have been through robberies, teacher turnover, staff changes, now COVID-19 (Coronavirus)."

We had to ACT immediately!

My principal gave us the rules:

1. Set up Verge (a program made by DCSD that I never used)
2. Use ClassDojo for all communication needs
3. Set up Google Voice for all calls and translations (Did I mention we are a school with over 100 different languages?!?!)
4. Discuss with your team what you plan to do regarding teaching students over the next two weeks.

My team met briefly; we were all baffled by this. The only thing we could do was provide our students with packets until we came up with a better plan for effectively teaching them, and we were told when we could return. I pray this virus will last for two weeks, and we can return to normal.

Virtual Learning! Are You Serious? **3/20/2020**

Yup! It was hell!! See, all this time, my students picked up packets weekly from the bin with a first-grade tag from outside the building. Then, we received a message from our principal stating that we were using too much paper and would have to begin teaching virtually.

Lives were changing drastically in just a week. People were getting sick and dying, parents became teachers overnight, and kids lost stability as well as socialization.

Me!?!?! Well, I was, of course, all over the place, and now my anxiety was up the roof! I was not only working from home, which I was not used to, but I was now creating assignments on Verge, Dojo, and email, along with helping my 8th grader with his work. My youngest son was on the verge of graduating and attending high school. The school he attended had unreal expectations. The workload given to the student was ridiculous, and it was way too much to try to keep up with him and my students. My house became an all-hands-on-deck situation. Everyone, including my 80-plus-year-old grandmother, had a job to do.

Schools were trying to figure out a schedule using the computer as the leading platform. We were told we had to use Microsoft Teams as our online tool. I have never used Teams. Here I am, training myself to use Teams before we start online teaching. Through all of this, my phone rang nonstop, and the parents asked how to complete the assignments in the work packet, how I would grade the assignments, and when the assignments were due. I was exhausted and not only did we have to deal with all the parent requests, but we also had meetings ALL THE TIME!!!

Lord help me!

Our New Schedule **3/23/20**

So, this week, I decided that for this to work, I must get organized. I had to be organized at home and at work. I created a school schedule, my personal schedule, and a schedule for my child.

All my schedules were posted in my new classroom, a guest room in my house with a table, portable whiteboard, erasers, webcam, computer, mouse, curriculum books, and several notebooks.

Sunday–Friday (my teacher's/personal schedule)

Sunday—All work will be posted on Class Dojo. This will be our main platform for students to access work and Teams, where we will have face-to-face class sessions. Make sure I take a long bath, drink wine, and create ME time!

Monday-Friday

- 7 a.m.—Log in, check emails, and read Dojo messages
- 8:00–9:30 a.m.—Take any questions about workload from parents via Teams before class starts
- 10:00–11:00 a.m.—Take a brain break and grade assignments from the previous week
- 11:00 a.m.–12:00 p.m.—Email check and contact parents to see if any assistance is needed
- 12:00–1:00 p.m.—Lunchtime. Take a walk around the neighborhood/LOG OFF
- 1:00–2:00 p.m.—Log on to the computer
- 2:00–3:00 p.m.—Close out our Teams class session, give students an encouraging message on Class Dojo with a recap of our day and expectations for the next school day, along with our Computer Rules
- 3:00–4:00 p.m.—Teacher planning time, keep the computer in my new teacher's room, close out Dojo (now I have it scheduled and cannot receive any messages until the next school day), and lock my

Google Voice number it was expected to be on voice mail only until the next day at 6 a.m.

Students schedule:

- 7:50–8:30 a.m.—Students log in and attend Specials
- 8:30–10:00 a.m.—Math review
- 8:30–8:50 a.m.—Daily review
- 8:50–9:00 a.m.—Fact Practice using YouTube or Fact Dash from our math curriculum
- 9:00–10:00 a.m.—Daily assignments using our math curriculum. I would screenshot the pages and create assignments on Dojo. Students would go to their Dojo portfolio to find the assignment. I would share my screen to teach the assignment. We would work collaboratively on the first page, the second page would be independent practice, and the final page would be a screenshot of their homework.
- 10:00 a.m.–2:15 p.m.—ELA (reading was much more difficult. We did not have a real curriculum for reading, and most of the assignments were Teachers Pay Teachers worksheets that became my go-to! Thank you, TPT!!!
    - 10:00–10:20 a.m.—ELA Review (phonics sounds using YouTube)
    - 10:20–10:40 a.m.—Read the book of the day from GetEpic, and students complete the comprehension questions
    - 10:40–11:10 a.m.—Comprehension questions and worksheet. Screenshots of the worksheet were posted in ClassDojo
    - 11:10 a.m.–12:00 p.m.—Daily ELA assignments and writing
    - 12:00–12:30 p.m.—Lunch
    - 12:30–12:45 p.m.—Student Free Time- Students use this time to go outside for recess and take a break from the computer
    - 12:45–1:30 p.m.—Social Studies would show a video and use our Social Studies Weekly assignments to teach the students. Studies Weekly was a lifesaver!!

    - 1:30–2:15 p.m.—Science: This was difficult because we didn't have a steady science curriculum that used an online platform. Most of the time, I would use videos on YouTube and have students create STEM activities using resources they have around the house. This was truly the kids' favorite time of the day!
- 2:15 p.m.—I would end class and use this time to talk to parents about any questions or concerns they might have.

Having an ESOL class, I had to provide videos using platforms such as YouTube and GetEpic to help students see what they were learning, especially first graders. GetEpic was my favorite reading resource because the comprehension questions were graded for you. This made grading so easy for a teacher like me!

MyMath was also a fantastic resource. Students already had their workbooks, and most of the time, I would upload the assignments in the Dojo and use the videos with the resources to help teach the lesson. Students learned how to take pictures of their homework and upload them to the Dojo to get credit for doing their homework.

Dojo was our primary platform for collecting and providing assignments, communicating with parents, and rewarding students. I would also mail students prizes with the highest Dojo points, or if it was their birthday. They loved getting a prize in the mail!

Parents go to Infinite Campus to get students' grades, and the DCDS website is a great resource for school updates and information on where parents can get free lunch from various bus stop locations.

So now that I have my school schedule, let's discuss my youngest son's schedule, which was a whole situation. I was not only a parent of a middle schooler, but I was also a parent of a child with an IEP for dyslexia, anxiety, and ADHD. Having a son with ADHD and being on the computer all day was not what I needed at this time in my life. This was way too much for me as a parent and for him as my child, now a student. A schedule was needed for us to maintain our sanity and relationship as mom and child. Rules were established, and if they weren't followed, his phone would be taken for the day; if you know a middle schooler, you know having their phone is life, especially during quarantine!

Here is how my son's day went:

- 8:00 a.m.—Wake up, brush your teeth, wash your face, and wear an appropriate shirt, but pajama pants can stay on.
- 9:00 a.m.—Breakfast and setting up his computer area for school. This area was separated from his bedroom so he would not lie down while on the computer!
- 10:00–11:15 a.m.—ELA (complete assignments for the day and meet with the teacher via Zoom)
- 11:15 a.m.–12:00 p.m.—Connections

During this time, my son was in ROTC (Reserve Officer Training Corps) and did not like it. I could truly understand why he hated the class, but I also started to hate it with all the work this teacher gave on the computer. But my he never knew, lol.

- 12:00–1:00 p.m.—Break Time and walk to our neighborhood clubhouse for fresh air and conversation
- 1:00–2:00 p.m.—Math: This was a class I didn't like either, so my husband and older son had to help with this one. I'm a first-grade teacher; what do I know about middle school math?
- 2:00–3:00 p.m.—Social Studies and Science time

Since my son had an IEP, his teachers provided many videos and held extra Zoom sessions for tutorials on homework and class assignments. I liked how most of his work was on the entire district's platform, and the students were already familiar with navigating it. My son's school district was very organized, but they were known for excessive workloads, and many parents complained about this. The grading system was never modified, and students' test percentages were 45% of the grade.

Even though this was a very hectic time, my son did very well with virtual learning. Having the schedule helped him stay organized and allowed some flexibility, especially when his assignments were completed, and he did not have anything scheduled. It took a village to help him succeed, and he ended school with As, Bs, and 1Cs. We were very proud and hated that the pandemic interrupted his eighth-grade year.

The Week Before Spring Break! **3/30/20**

WOOHOO! Now that my youngest was on spring break, I could focus on my work schedule. This was when my district changed everything regarding our schedules. We were now having more PD sessions and were given Wednesday as a day to focus on grading, tutorial sessions, and planning. No virtual sessions were held on this day, and I loved it!

I have become very familiar with Teams and learned how to put assignments and announcements and use the whiteboard to help my students see what's being taught in real-time. My first-grade team created a learning menu that included the days and the links we would use to help students gain access to their work. This learning menu was given out the week before, so parents knew the learning expectations. Each teacher was responsible for putting in the work for their subject. This collaborative effort shortened some of our planning time and gave teachers only one subject to focus on. This worked until I realized I would need to change some things due to how my students were learning virtually. At times, one teacher may have been further ahead than others or may not use the same resources due to how their students learn on the computer. Now that the template was given, minor changes were made to ensure the work was more conducive to the needs of my students.

I also noticed something else: Parents were beginning to check out, and many of my students weren't attending class. My attendance was horrible, and my students' showed signs of burnout. I knew then, it was time for SPRING BREAK!

CHAPTER TWO

SELF-LOVE AND SCHEDULES

We Are Back **4/13/20**

Spring break was needed for all of us! During spring break, I realized I needed to add more self-care to my day. I started meditating more, working out more, therapy sessions with Better Help to adjust to being quarantined, meeting with friends on Wednesdays to have social distancing dinners, and sitting outside to do my work. My husband and I became creative with date night ideas to help me with my social media addiction. I also began learning how to cook new recipes by watching YouTube. Prayer lines on Monday and Wednesday helped with my spiritual faith, and every Sunday, I attended church online. I had to find new ways to make myself happy. I was becoming more and more anxious about work and the number of deaths we were facing in our country. Feeling overwhelmed with the pandemic, I was no longer myself and didn't like the person I was becoming. I had to get myself together mentally and not allow the pandemic to take over my mental health.

This was my new beginning in just one week of spring break with my family, and now, we are back to digital learning. GEESH!

My son's school district was starting to annoy me; this was when the school superintendent mandated that the teachers in that district come in and teach the students virtually from the classroom. It was so sad! So many protests were happening, and petitions were being signed, and you already know, callouts were being made. I have learned that many people were being exposed for who they are, and our country was unprepared! We saw so much lack of compassion, leadership, and empathy from our leaders. There was little unity, and many were left to fend for themselves. There was such a lack of direction!

Now that I have this off my chest, let's get back to school stuff!!!

Another New Schedule **4/20/20**

Well, we received news that we have yet another new schedule! But this time I LOVED IT! So, Monday was science, Tuesday was specials, Wednesday was ELA and Social Studies, Thursday was parent conferences and tutorials, and Friday was a teacher workday! What a relief!!! This means we focused on one subject at a time, and students and teachers had less screen time.

Every Tuesday at 9 a.m., my grade level and I meet with our instructional support team. The purpose of these meetings was to ensure we collaborated on our lesson plans, received the resources we needed to be effective, discussed concerns we might have, and gathered any updates from our principal and the county. I appreciate my principal having more small group meetings; staff meetings were only held as needed. Fewer meetings were GREAT FOR ME!

The cons of our small group meetings were that they only focused on guided reading. We talked so much about guided reading, and I didn't understand the purpose because we weren't doing much guided reading at this time. I felt we should have focused more on the digital learning platform, resources for all subjects, and how we can continue to support our students and parents virtually.

Smooth Sailing **4/27/20**

Well, now we are officially in the groove. My parents knew exactly what to do, and I was way more confident with digital learning and using a variety of resources to help my students succeed. Parent conferences were short and brief, and work packets were available at the school for students with technical difficulties. I created a spreadsheet to help me see my students' grades and the parents I needed to contact.

Student Name	Date
KL	Read-100 Science-90 SS-90 Math-90
MD	WP (work packet)
ST	VM-Voice Mail (no work)
TM	N/A-Parent and child unavailable
DF	Read-80 Science-70 Math-PC (parent contact/no work) SS-90

WP- Work Packet given
VM-Voice Mail to a parent about work
N/A- Parent and Student unavailable this week
PC-Parent Contact regarding missing grade

This spreadsheet was a great way for me to hold parents and students accountable for assignments. I also sent a copy to the parents via email or Dojo so they could have it before I posted any grades in Infinite Campus.

Working from 8:45 a.m. to 1:45 p.m. allowed me to get more done throughout my day. We were also told that the last school day was changed from May 21st to May 15!!! OHHH YEAH!!!

To Retain or Not Retain **5/4/20**

So, this week, we were told the grading system will change due to the pandemic! Here we go, another change. One thing about being a teacher during the pandemic is that you must be flexible! New students will keep the grades they had pre-COVID. Assignments given after the pandemic and when digital learning began would be considered enrichment grades or grade boosters. For example, If TM had an F in ELA before the pandemic, his assignments during the pandemic would help his grade and help him pass the class. Also, my district discouraged any failing grades unless it was due to extreme circumstances. If TM failed with an F in ELA before the pandemic and did not complete any of the assignments during the pandemic, then the teacher had to judge retention.

Teachers also had to show documentation that parents were contacted about the grades daily, and this documentation must be in Infinite Campus. Teachers also had to show how they tried to help the students not fail. What resources were given? Were tutorial sessions provided? How much remediation was done, and how did you help the parent help their child be successful? This was truly a lot! If you choose to retain a student, a meeting will occur virtually with the teacher, parent, assistant principal, ESOL teacher (if necessary), and grade-level chair. Based on the meeting and documentation, it was determined whether the student would be retained. So, as you can tell, all my students passed first grade. It was tough to retain students at this time. The argument of the pandemic, lack of technical resources, and parents making so many adjustments predicted that the students would be promoted.

It's a Wrap! **5/11/20**

This was the last week of school, and parents, students, and teachers were thrilled. This was truly a stressful year. Parents were yelling, "Give teachers raises! Being in quarantine, teachers were getting a lot of recognition for what we do. The World News even recognized teachers for being so creative during unprecedented times. Teachers showed up in so many ways to support their students and parents. Finally, you saw administrators and teachers working together to ensure students feel supported and acknowledged for overcoming the most challenging situation they could ever face.

Teachers created farewell parades, and drive-byes became popular for any occasion. Banners were placed at the students' front doors to congratulate them for making it. I liked what this principal from Texas did. Despite not having a proper graduation service, he went to each graduating senior's house and delivered yard signs to wish them the best and let them know they were loved.

Tele graduations were HUGE during this time! Celebrities showed up by giving so many scholarships and cash app payments to the class of 2020. In my house, we celebrated my youngest son's completion of 8th grade! We had a drive-by, stop-by outside celebration that was a HUGE Success!!! It was so special; my son felt much love from his family and friends.

I hate that this class had to endure so much, but one thing is sure: This class will always be known as resilient, overcomers, and unique. They will always be remembered!

CHAPTER THREE

SUMMER LIT

Teacher Work Week 2020 **6/3/20**

Now that the kids were gone for the summer, the county had to decide how we would come back to clean classrooms and close out the school year. This week, we didn't do anything but have virtual meetings and wait until an email was sent on how we could go back into the building. I was truly ready for summer break. My mind was cluttered; mentally and physically, I was tired and overwhelmed.

When we finally received the email from the county, which took several weeks for them to decide, teachers were given a staggered schedule on how to come in and clean our classrooms. I was genuinely excited about this moment. I could not wait to see the class. I had to leave abruptly in March. I was also happy to receive an offer to teach virtual summer school. This was my first-year teaching reading camp. I would use all the tools and resources I learned throughout my digital learning experience. Looking back at this situation, I know everything I learned will be helpful to me for years.

Schedules were finally posted, and grade levels could enter the building around 8:30 a.m. to pack students' belongings. We had to use this week only to pack students' belongings, get students' devices returned, and give parents summer bridge materials for continuous summer learning. When I entered the building, I was mandated to wear a mask and stay 6 feet away from anyone else. My classroom looked the same way as I left it. Students' desks were grouped in pairs of 6, my teacher's desk was tucked in the corner, a rug on the floor, the library area was set up with cozy pillows, a kidney table for small groups, and students' cubbies with some of their belongings still left inside them. I just stood there and looked around at what used to be a functioning classroom. I immediately put on my gloves and used bleach as I cleaned the students' desks. Being a teacher for many years, students hide anything in their desks, which can be disgusting! My principal gave directions on how to store students' books, coats, and anything else they left, and where to place all the desks in the classroom. Three different checklists, distributing students' belongings to parents on a drive-by day, and cleaning out our classrooms had to be completed in three days. I prioritized using day one to clean my class thoroughly and move all furniture to the back of the room. On day 2, we had parents drive-by day, during which each grade level had a specific time that parents came through the car rider lane to return Chromebooks and pick up student items—this day disappointed me because I had two parents show up out of 21 students. I think the schedule may not have worked with parents' work schedules, and there were opportunities during the summer for parents to return items as well. I was hurt because I wanted to give my students a proper goodbye. Teachers were free to go once all items were completed on the checklist and signed off by the administrators. Well, I guess that's it for me! Summer School, here I come!

Summer school turned out to be a fantastic experience. We were assigned ten students from various schools in the district to attend online learning. I was blessed to be able to teach first grade during summer lit camp. This was the grade I was used to and very familiar with. Our reading resource came from Scholastic Literacy Pro, which was simple to use and navigate, and easy for the students to use. I also liked the way I could see how many minutes they completed outside of camp hours. My site director came from another school in the county, and he was cool. My favorite part about him was that he did not believe in long meetings. He was straight to the point and had an open-door (or open computer, lol) policy. He was available anytime. Summer school was only for 9 days, and our hours were from 8:00 a.m. to 12:00 p.m. (morning routine), 12:00 p.m. to 1:00 p.m. (lunch), and 1:00 p.m. to 2:00 p.m. (afternoon/dismissal). Students were given a core value of the day to reflect on. Students learned about friendship, courage, kindness, hope, and compassion. Each core value had a book for the lesson, a PowerPoint presentation, and a camp song. Students were given assessments so teachers could see where they were in their reading levels, and comprehension activities were also given to help students with critical thinking.

We started our day every morning at 8 a.m. on Teams with our morning meeting and camp song. We would transition into our core value and book of the day, where students use this time to talk about how the core value resonated with them. Once story time was over, students were given directions to do independent reading time, where they could read anywhere in their home, but must use the Literacy Pro platform so I could see their reading minutes. Specials were also offered for my students; they virtually attended music or PE each day. We had some cool specials teachers, who made specials a lot of fun for the kids. We would complete a phonics activity and recap what we had learned.

On the last day, I was saddened that our time together was ending so soon. I grew to form a bond with my summer school students and parents. It is crazy how you can connect with students and not be physically with each other. I also learned a valuable lesson while teaching summer lit camp. During my entire time teaching, I did not know I was teaching a district administrator's child, who held an important position within the district. She gave me so much praise for my teaching style and told me she would say a good word to the summer coordinator about how great I was and how attentive I was with my online students. The lesson in this is "Do your job and do it effectively; you never know who may be watching and how connections are made. When you are kind and work hard, you never know what is in store."

CHAPTER FOUR

BACK AT IT

Summer Where? **08/03/20**

Wow! This has been an enjoyable summer but we are back at it. The Coronavirus is at an all-time high, and the death toll continues to rise. So many people are being infected, and I have never been as scared as I am today. No real mandates are being put in place, and now, we are using the words "strongly encouraged" when wearing a mask. Social distancing is barely there, and people are out like nothing is happening.

Schools are in limbo, and parents are protesting for schools to reopen while teachers are protesting for schools to remain closed and stay virtual until the numbers decrease. We were told that funding would be taken away if schools do not reopen. Everything seems so crazy!

We finally heard from several districts about what they would do about opening schools. Some schools chose to stay virtual, while others opened and allowed parents to select virtual learning. One county decided to open virtually for only two weeks, and at the end of August, all students and teachers were to enter the building through a phased system. Another county opened with no option of virtual teaching; the hallways were extremely crowded with students, and no masks were worn. This county went viral, and pictures of the students were posted on all social media outlets, causing a lot of conversation about the health and safety of the kids. The school superintendent stated that the picture taken was out of context and that it was only one part of the school. Students weren't mandated to wear masks, but it was strongly encouraged. The student who posted that picture was suspended the next day. SMH! Her suspension did not last long due to the influx of messages and social media posts defending the student. We were living in a sad situation.

Many counties returned to school as if the situation was normal, and schools closed left and right due to high case numbers. So, students were in and out of school for weeks.

My county decided to remain virtual but tried to furlough our pay for nine days. After several protests and teacher uproars, we were only furloughed for one day. We were also given a three-day learning institute program that provided resources and ways to teach effectively using a remote platform. This institute provided stipends for teachers and was not mandated. It was a great way to make up for that one furlough day.

I was blessed with the position of first-grade and grade-level chair during these unprecedented times in education. In our first leadership meeting, we had a detailed discussion of how we would look when our school finally opened. This meeting lasted hours, and no matter how much planning we did, we still weren't ready for what was to come.

First-Grade Vibes **08/10/20**

My first week as a first-grade teacher and grade-level chair. I answered many questions, solved many problems, and tackled many situations. This position has many challenges, but I am truly thankful to my first-grade team for stepping in and helping me overcome some of our obstacles. This week, we were in daily meetings focusing on our virtual teaching. We also had an open house this week during our daily meetings. We were stressed out, but my principal was flexible and listened to the needs of the teachers. She provided accommodations throughout the week to help alleviate some of the stress we were experiencing.

Teachers were in limbo about which learning platform to use to help instruct the students. Are we using Google Classroom, Verge, Zoom, or Teams? There were no clear directions on using these platforms or which one the county required. I made personal phone calls to my team to see if they were okay and check their mental state. I called my parents to remind them of the Open House and to sign up for Class Dojo so they could stay in the know. I wish there were more interpreters available for our students and parents. My school has a large population of EL students, and we need translators to help us during the first week of school to eliminate misconceptions. I wish DeKalb had drive-through lanes with several translators in different languages so parents could drive up, speak to the interpreter, get the paperwork they needed for their child, and sign up for Dojo. This would have been a lifesaver!

Moving on to Open House! We discovered pre-k-2nd would not use Chromebooks during the first two weeks of school. We would use packets while teaching virtually. All copies need to be made before Open House on Thursday. We received the news that the packets had to be ready by Monday! UGHH! So, my team and I split the responsibilities up. Each team member focused on a specific subject, found the worksheets, and uploaded them to SharePoint to send to our AP to make copies for our students.

On Tuesday, we met as a grade level to discuss what we would present to our parents for Open House and complete our mandated modules for the county. In the middle of my meeting, I heard a loud BOOM outside. I ran to my door, looked outside, and was told by my neighbor that the transformer blew! I was immediately blocked from getting back on my computer. My internet was out, and the lights, too! Whyyyyyy!!!!!!

We were given a schedule on Wednesday with staggered arrival times for distributing student packets and Chromebooks. I was the first to go to school from 8:00 to 10:00 a.m. First grade was in the front of the school, and third grade met in the cafeteria. When I arrived, everything was so organized. You rang the bell to get into the school, and a security officer was there to open the door, check your temperature, and give you gloves and a mask. On the way to my AP tables, teachers were given back-to-school gifts. We stopped at the bookkeeper's table for chart paper, folders, copy paper, pens, and other office supplies. As I walked to my classroom, I opened my door to see a clear classroom with all my desks pushed to the side of the room. It felt good to see my classroom, and I must say I missed being in the building.

When it was time to distribute materials, parents would drive up to receive their students' items. Teachers were inside sorting materials while teachers outside greeted parents and handed out the student resources. If a child was not on our class list, they had to park, go to the front office, and become fully registered using the parent center. Due to COVID, students did not need complete documentation to attend school, and no students were to be turned away; all students received a Chromebook and had to sign a contract. Damaged and unreturned Chromebooks consist of a $300 fee.

The admin team had everything in order. I just wish there were more interpreters in our building to assist.

That evening, we had to host a virtual open house, which my team and I worked very hard to put together. Our PowerPoint had our Bitmojis as if we were with the parents, presenting necessary information for the school term. The Bitmoji was also a representation of what the teacher had to show on a specific slide. The open house turned out well, and we had over 50 parents attend. There were a lot of instructions, and we sent out the presentation to all parents as a resource tool to assist with any questions they may have.

TGIF! This was training day and Chromebook distribution. We had four people to assist with this task, and the computers were labeled with the student's name and separated by grade level (3–5). All parents had to do was drive up and give their child's teacher's name, and we would distribute materials while my principal marked them on the computer. Parents needing K-2 materials would go to the front office and look in their specific grade bin for student packets and books.

A lot was accomplished this week, and school will begin next week!!!

Tech Issues **08/17/2020**

It was the first week of school, and of course, it was exciting. Our entire technology system crashed on Monday and Tuesday, and none of our tech resources from the county were available. There were so many tech issues!!! Microsoft Teams was giving us all kinds of trouble, and I had to message my parents to use an alternative platform, Zoom. I was so grateful that K-2 was using work packets, and I answered all questions using email, Dojo, and phone. Our packets and books were available for all parents and students who needed resources all week. We also had lunch provided at the school for students in need.

This week was about getting to know each other virtually and learning the platforms we will use to complete instruction. I told the parents we would use Zoom until all students could receive their Chromebooks. Once students get their computers, we will switch to Microsoft Teams. We will also go from work packets to our online platform, Verge.

Each day, we worked on a new skill in our packet, which included two weeks of work for every subject. I was pleased that all 22 first-grade students attended our Zoom session daily. Another great benefit was that almost all my students were returning from kindergarten and were familiar with using computers and online platforms. This week, we focused on student expectations, virtual class rules, our schedule, and motivational rewards. The county made Monday and Tuesday half days for the first couple of weeks, which was great, especially with all the tech issues we faced.

My students enjoyed the first week of school, and their favorite part was earning the highest Dojo to have virtual lunch with me! I noticed they worked so hard to accomplish that goal. Virtual lunch allowed me to converse with the students and learn more about their needs, wants, likes, and dislikes. It turned out to be my favorite part of the day as well!

On Wednesdays, my principal always had "Is everything okay" meetings to discuss what we needed to improve. This was our round table for teachers to vent their issues. In this pandemic, I have learned that communication is key!

Flexible Teaching **08/24/2020**

Okay, we're finally making improvements!! My parents were now used to getting online, using Zoom, and accessing our work packets. I would post what was needed for class on Dojo so students were prepared, and list times for bathroom breaks so no instruction was missed.

This week, many parents complained about not having adequate technology. There should be no reason why K-2 was without Chromebooks. Due to all the complaints, the parents' concerns were answered, and Chromebooks were available for the parents to drive by the school and pick up the next day.

Now that students have their computers, I had to be flexible and change my instruction to show my students how to use the Chromebook and access Teams. We were no longer using Zoom, and students needed to know two things: 1. How to get on the call and 2. Where can we find work? The county also threw in a code of conduct training that we had to give the students, which was an entire mess! Students had to listen to me read the code of conduct PPT and take a test after each module! Now, I have been figuring out how this would work with first graders, who were getting their computers for the first time and still learning how to use them! I always wonder who makes these decisions in the district office and whether they consider the little ones. I had to take two days from our regular scheduled instruction to complete the code of conduct PowerPoint and quizzes. I had to find an incentive to get this done, so I gave Dojo points to all students who completed the Code of Conduct quizzes!! SMH!

Wednesdays were also my day for parent meetings. This was the time for me to receive parental feedback, talk about our platforms, provide homework help, and address any other questions or concerns they may have. This Wednesday, I was swamped with meetings! I was exhausted from my parents, staff, and leadership meetings.

On Thursday, I decided to record videos on how to use Chromebooks, access all our platforms, and use the various features on Teams. I put all the videos on Dojo and told parents to refer to them whenever they needed assistance. This was a lifesaver in alleviating all the calls and questions.

It was finally Friday, and something alarming happened! One of my teammates became seriously ill, and we had to come up with a plan for her virtual students. We decided to split her students amongst the team and send our own Teams links for them to come to our classes. We also became co-teachers in her Dojo to help give parents the communication they need to continue student learning. Teachers must go with the flow and roll with the punches!

Virtual Observations REALLY? **08/31/20**

Okay, we are seeing the light! FINALLY! So, my students were now acclimated to Teams and accessing their work. Parents knew the rules and expectations, so our Wednesday meetings were a breeze. I still had students from my teammates' class who were settled. Everything was going so well until I read my email. It's time for teacher observations! Observations include our AP, academic coach, and principal. MY GOD! You must be kidding! How?! We just started school!?!

During observations, the admin team logged into my Teams platform and watched me teach my students a math lesson. Everything went well until my computer glitched, and my internet went in and out. UGGGGHHHH! My students were exceptional, though. They told the admin team, "It's okay; don't leave. Mrs. Sessom will be back; she is just glitching." LOLOLOL! I love first grade!

I met with my academic coach on Friday to discuss my observation. She told me she had to bring her boss from the district on the line to watch me teach my students, and he wanted to give me huge kudos for creating one of the best virtual classes in the district.

WOOHOO! This was the news I needed to hear! He enjoyed how I had all my tabs up and organized, making my lessons available with no wait time; I used Verge to store my lessons, controlled the mute button for minimal distractions, and my students were highly engaged.

I was so happy that I sent my parents and students a huge shout-out and gave them all a virtual lunch session with me for the good report!

CHAPTER FIVE

CURRICULUM NIGHT AND ASSESSMENTS! REALLY!

Upgrade ME **09/07/2020**

I needed Labor Day! One day made a significant difference in my mental health. Like the previous weeks, everything went well, and my new internet Wi-Fi was much better. So, before the pandemic, we never understood the impact of having an upgraded internet speed. We went from 25 to 800. I am zooming through my lessons.

This week, my students were very engaged. They were getting better and better. Wednesday was meeting day, and it interfered with my RTI sessions with my students. This year, I have one student needing intervention and assistance. He was having a hard time learning the letters of the alphabet, and if you are in education, you know the only way a student can get evaluated is through documentation. Now that COVID has interfered with education, it has become even harder to get the documentation needed for my student because the county has put a hold on student evaluations. This was NOT GOOD! That means when it is time to evaluate students, they will either go undiagnosed or have a backlog of paperwork for all parties involved in the evaluation process.

The highlight of my week was Friday, when I had a parent meeting to update my parents on what's going on with school, COVID procedures, changes that would occur in class, and any questions or concerns they may have. In this specific meeting, I had to let my parents know we will have a different start time next week for announcements, and small group sessions will begin right after. At the end of the meeting, a parent stated she was very thankful for me and the patience I have displayed so far with this online learning. Things have been so hard, especially when parents have multiple children, and it feels good when you have a teacher who makes the student independent and keeps parents in the know. Words like this make the job all worth it!

It's My Birthday **9/14/2020**

It's my birthday week, and curriculum night is the same day as my birthday! This week, my team and I focused on what we will present for curriculum night and how we will discuss our new way of teaching students using the standards.

Wednesday's staff meeting was now in the morning due to curriculum night being that night. We discussed the upcoming assessments students will take, along with the grading period that is coming up. I was in disbelief that we were still grading students in such trying times. It just doesn't make sense that students had to get grades while trying to cope with a new way of learning. Around noon, I had a grade-level meeting to do a mock curriculum presentation and review any kinks. Our meeting started at 11:15 a.m. and ended at 1:40 p.m. Curriculum night started at 4:30! ON MY BIRTHDAY!!!

I have been working all day preparing our slides, teaching students, attending meetings, giving mock presentations, discussing the needs of the ESOL students for curriculum nights, and contacting parents to remind them to attend.

4:30 came around so fast, and it was time to present to our parents. I created a new channel for the parents to log into for curriculum night, and I displayed our PowerPoint presentation so that parents could see it when they entered the meeting. I thought I was prepared until my principal told us she would have PTA night before our curriculum night! WHAT! So now I had to tell all the parents to go to another link for PTA night and then return to our link for curriculum night. It was an actual disaster. Parents were all over the place. So, I had to stay on my curriculum night channel to guide parents to the PTA channel. My frustration level was at an all-time high!

After my principal presented her messages, budget, intro to all the teaching staff, and virtual learning sessions, it was time for parents to return to our channel for curriculum night. At this point, I was ready for the day to end. Parents were at other grade-level curriculum night channels; they had difficulty getting into their grade-level channel, and many ended up leaving due to all the confusion. After all that work my team and I did for curriculum night, we had four parents on our channel for the entire grade level to show up. We told our parents we would post our presentation on Dojo for parents to refer to, too. This was a huge disaster; again, did I mention it was my BIRTHDAY!

Friday was another day of tech glitches, even with my new Wi-Fi. I kept getting kicked out of Teams. My assignments weren't posted, and I was notified that Teams was glitching. I had to end class at 11:30 a.m., tell my students to work independently, go to lunch, and try to meet again at 1:00 p.m.

When we returned at 1:00 p.m., Teams finally decided to work. We ended our session with a special visit from our school counselor, who spoke about ways to balance screen time. School ended early that day, and I got my lesson plans, grades, and all other tasks done by 3:00!

Maintaining My Mental Health **9/21/2020**

It's self-care Monday, continuing from self-care Sunday. Which I now make part of my daily routine. I find ways to incorporate some self-care into my routine, no matter what. So, I decided that today was a good day to take off. I am a true believer in listening to my mind and body. I was starting to feel depleted, drained, and exhausted. I needed to take care of myself and disconnect from all technology. I was beginning to feel like my computer was taking over me. My cell phone became addictive, and I was tired of the routine. So, I texted my AP and first-grade team and told them I would not be online today. I sent my students and parents a Dojo message to have them work independently on various assignments, and we will discuss them on Tuesday. I took this time to rest and slept until after 1:00 p.m. I felt so much better. I woke up, didn't turn on the TV, didn't pick up my phone, kept the lights off, and meditated. I spent much-needed quality time with my husband. My husband surprised me and told me to hop in the car. We did something I had never done before: we rode around the city with no real destination. It felt so good to leave my phone at home and do something spontaneous. We ate ice cream, walked around a park, and talked for hours. I felt PEACE.

When I arrived home, I sat in my backyard, played music, and wrote in my journal. I needed to take care of myself! This was necessary, and I realized that I am not suitable for anyone if I don't take care of myself first. ME TIME is ESSENTIAL!

Well, it's Tuesday, and yes, I am back online with my students! They missed me in just one day and couldn't believe I took off. When I finished teaching my online class for the day, I received an email stating that we would take the MAP assessment next week and be prepared to go to training and watch videos on administering the test. REALLY!!!!! Why are we testing students and not getting the real data we need to see where students are when we know the parents are in the background giving answers? SMH! At this point, I was over everything! The constant meetings, training, videos, inconsistency, lack of organization, and constant changes. Nothing ever made sense, and we were always put in a predicament where we had to be flexible and overcome a new challenge. It was becoming taxing on me mentally.

I-Ready and MAP 9/28/2020

This week, we will administer the i-Ready assessments in math and reading. I-Ready was one of the resources we used to create and assign assignments to our students to target their strengths and weaknesses. The resource was also good at monitoring progress and collecting student data in the RTI process.

The test was split into two days, and students had to turn their screens on and mute them. This was my way of seeing students' tests. It's crazy that on the first day of testing, the parents were on the screen trying to help their children, and I also had a parent taking the actual diagnostic assessment. How will this work, and we haven't administered MAP yet? I couldn't believe all the issues I was having with a simple test, such as Iready.

Students had their screens on and speakers on mute. As we were testing, I saw parents in the background. I had one student keep turning his screen on and off. I had another student tell me their screen suddenly wasn't working. SMH!

I had to keep reminding parents to allow their children to do their best. This was a test to help me see student data; it was not a test for any grade in class. But, of course, that went in one ear and out the other. Do you know that after all that testing, I still had students who just sat there, did nothing on their computers, and just let the test run?

THIS WAS A BUSTED WEEK!

CHAPTER SIX

TESTING, TESTING, AND MORE TESTING

Pop-up Blocker Issues **10/05/20**

Well, this week was MAP assessment week! SMH! I thought i-Ready was a mess; this was something I had never planned for in my entire life. Everything was all over the place. So, the night before, I sent a schedule to my parents. I decided to test 4–5 students a day since we had a week to complete the reading assessment and a week to complete the math, which would be next week. I put the website on our Clever page for easy access for students. I sent several reminders to parents on Dojo about getting plenty of rest, eating a healthy meal, and being prepared for the test without parental support.

Monday was testing day, and my phone went off like crazy when my teacher friends told me the testing session was an entire mess. So, I set up a private testing channel for our Teams and made it private for only the students I wanted to test. On our general channel, I was blessed to have a student teacher to help the other students with their assignments. I sent plenty of work to Dojo and made a list of students who had missing assignments to complete while I focused on testing. As I called in my first testing group into the channel, I was given 45 minutes to focus on the testing session, and we could test in the morning, but my gut told me to include the afternoon as well. I'm glad I listened to my gut, too!

My students had no issues getting to the website. The problem we faced was that every student was given a pop-up blocker notice to test, which was a complete disaster. We must remember I am testing students in first grade, and now I must instruct them on how to turn off their pop-up blocker. So, the instructions were for students to go to their computer, and in the privacy section of settings was the pop-up blocker on and off key. This was not only a task for first graders, but I also tried to explain it to parents who do not speak English. I am grateful I started with my gifted group first, and they didn't have any issues at all. I am also thankful I had two students who could do this task independently. I had so many students who needed help from their parents, and I had to have my instructional coach and even the ESOL teacher help me. This was an all-hands-on-deck situation that was very frustrating. I went from having eight students in my testing session to only being able to test 4, and now it's 10:30 a.m.

By the time I had my afternoon group, testing had gone smoother due to the heads-up I had given my parents and the assistance from my student teacher, who was teaching my group while I was in my testing session. I was also grateful that my instructional coach sent a PowerPoint to help parents understand how to turn off the pop-up blocker. Of course, with all of this going on, an email came from my principal alerting the staff about an emergency meeting at 1:00 p.m. SMH!

My afternoon session was more productive, and I could test more than five kids. Students had to keep their screens on and use the mute button. Parents were to leave the room to allow students to test, and many of my parents did not follow the rules. Today was crazy!

Make-Up Testing mixed with Exhaustion 10/12/20

I am officially over-testing; I was exhausted, and it was only October. We had one day off due to Columbus Day, and I noticed our calendar did not have many days off. Due to virtual classes, our school days became longer and tiring, and teachers were burned left and right. Since we were virtual, the expectation was to work harder, and I am confused as to why, when nothing was normal. Some tasks they wanted us to complete made no sense, and there were conversations about us returning to the building soon. With cases being so high and everyone getting sick or dying, I was becoming anxious. I would be in meetings at least three days a week. If it wasn't for leadership, it was for my grade level, and let's not forget I had to have conferences with parents weekly. I'm tired, and now I wonder if this job is for me anymore. I started to think about other jobs I could be doing that weren't so stressful, or maybe I could stay at home and tutor kids. I was growing weary of my profession, and I knew I had a passion for it, but it wasn't the same, and the value for teachers wasn't what it needed to be. The pay didn't equate to the amount of work and stress the job entailed. I was losing myself mentally, and I noticed I was becoming distant from my family because I was putting so much energy into others and losing focus on what mattered most. This job isn't for the weak; we must always be on. I know what it felt like to put on a mask when, deep down inside, I was suffering mentally. I had to figure out something soon and make it work for me if I was going to continue teaching.

Now that we are in week two of testing, math didn't go as badly. We fixed all the tech kinks from last week's testing, and now we are working on assessing students in math. Of course, the same rules were applied: parents were to leave the room while students tested, screens had to be on, and mics had to be muted. Again, many of my parents weren't listening. They were still in the room, and we had students with screen issues again. SMH!

I was glad testing was over, but next week was the make-up week, and plenty of students still had to make up their tests.

Town Hall Session 10/19/20

Map testing make-up week! I notified my parents to let them know who still needed to be tested. My ESOL teacher has been assigned to test all ESOL students, and it had to be done by 11/11. She had over 29 students to test, and I felt bad for her because this included students who had just come into the country. That was very difficult because many had to go through the pop-up blocker and could not speak English. This was terrible and unfortunate for the teacher, student, and parent.

I told the ESOL teacher to create a schedule and stick with it. Share the schedule with the parents and document everything. If a student was a no-show, document it; if the parent was sitting next to the student, document it; and if the pop-up blocker would not come off due to language barriers, document it. I also felt bad for the ESOL teacher because she had to test her 29 students, and the teacher's class, who was severely ill, had 24 students.

We also had our highly anticipated town hall meeting, where teachers sent questions to their teacher of the year in the building, and that person compiled all the questions and sent them to the Superintendent. The superintendent had several reps in this meeting, including HR reps, the COVID-19 task force, curriculum teams, the HVAC team, and wellness members. Each team presented a PPT to discuss their role and how they can assist teachers while working virtually. I also liked how each rep would take questions about their specific department. The meeting was clear and concise, summing up some misconceptions about going back into the building and what happens next. I like the fact that our new superintendent had this town hall meeting. It showed her level of communication and her desire to ensure a connection between her and the teaching staff. She wanted to give us the space to vent and express ourselves while keeping it organized and professional. Even though there may have been a few questions that I needed to know, I felt better knowing we were still going to be virtual, and at this point, there was no rush to go back into the buildings.

COVID and Halloween **10/26/2020**

This week, my computer has been glitching badly! I don't know if it was Teams or my Wi-Fi. I was constantly kicked out of Teams, couldn't share my screen, and the news was reporting a hurricane on Thursday.

When I have issues like this, it is easier for me to use asynchronous instruction to help my students stay on task with our weekly assignments. I would assign review assignments and contact the help desk to solve my issue while emailing my admin team about the problems I was facing with my technology.

On Wednesday, the news was hysterical about the projected tropical storm Zeta. It came from New Orleans, Alabama, and was supposed to hit north Georgia and the metro area. Grocery stores were packed, and schools were preparing to close or go virtual. My county decided to have no employees in the building, and all learning would be virtual, which meant nothing since we were already virtual.

Tropical Storm Zeta made her way to GA, and she came with a vengeance. Thousands were without power, my internet was down, and trees had fallen everywhere. Everything was a mess. I sent a Dojo message letting my students and parents know we will not meet virtually and to complete any missing assignments if possible. My parents were happy because many of them were without power as well. While sitting on my bed watching the news, a reporter came on the screen to warn us that many will be without power by Sunday! WHAT!!! SUNDAY!!! I took this as a blessing from GOD because I desperately needed rest and self-care.

Friday morning, many were still without power. I was blessed to have power, but my internet was still shaky. I assigned Halloween activities, went live for students who needed assistance, and ended the day early. I had so many students out due to the storm.

I felt so sorry for the kids this year; many could not trick or treat due to COVID-19. The news suggests parents get creative and have indoor parties with their immediate family to decrease exposure. Some other suggestions were to have a drive-by in the neighborhoods as well. It was sad to see kids not being able to do the things they were used to doing. In my neighborhood, many people had signs on their doors with “NO CANDY”. A few houses had candy at the front door with a “take one” sign. Churches hosted trick-or-treat outdoor celebrations, and one lady made an entire maze in her front yard for kids in her neighborhood to enjoy. People became creative and seeing that some kids could experience Halloween while others didn’t was sad. I went to my mom's house for our annual Halloween meet-up this year. She made the kids hot dogs, painted pumpkins, and ate cupcakes. It was cool and straightforward, as well as SAFE!

CHAPTER SEVEN

IS IT THANKSGIVING BREAK YET?

Election Time 11/2/2020

Well, it's election week, and President Biden Won! Many different views were presented during this time of the election, and we also had voters and our past President stating that the election was rigged. Several states were demanded to recount the votes, and some people working at the polls were getting threats. This was a crazy time. We also saw something we hadn't seen in years. GA turned BLUE! WOW! We also made history with VP Kamala Harris, the first African American female vice president. Due to the Stacy Abrams Foundation, thousands and thousands of African Americans came out to vote, and many were first-time voters. It was indeed a historic time.

After that historic day off, we were back at it, and finally, testing was completed. Even though I still had a few students to test, we were now moving on from that. Not much has changed; we were still working online, but now my county is discussing ways to get us back into the building. I knew this time was coming, and I was having mixed feelings. I was ready to leave my house, and teaching online was wearing on me, but I was also terrified of COVID-19 and have been lucky not to have gotten it, especially having an elder in my house.

This week, I had conferences with my parents and updated them on the growing conversation about returning to the building. I also gave parents resources on how students can protect themselves and what we will do as teachers to ensure their protection. We also had a board meeting to discuss the new CDC guidelines that allow the threshold to be under 200 instead of 100,000. Whatever it meant, I wasn't ready to face that we were heading back into the building!

Also, my principal was having us work on virtual data walls and data talk. I could not understand the purpose of having virtual data walls when the tests were invalid. The students either couldn't log on, or their parents were somewhere nearby. This was crazy! We were also going to use this data to create a virtual data wall, help with instruction, and create differentiated instruction virtually. This means lessons were to be tailored based on students' scores. I had some students' score gifted on the test, but they could not read! This is due to invalid data and parents being parents. At this point, the only instruction we should be given is basic. Students weren't listening online, and teachers were exhausted.

On strategy I really enjoyed to help keep students engaged my principal implemented was a virtual uniform dress code. Monday was NFL day, Tuesday was wearing your Idlewood Uniform, Thursday was appropriate PJ Day, and Friday was Spirit Wear. I also tried to dress up to keep the students excited about our virtual classroom learning.

Another strategy implemented was our virtual teachers' SWAP Day. At the end of each month, different teachers came on the line to discuss what they were great at while teaching virtually and share their teaching style. I had the honor of sharing my guided reading instruction and how I implement this instruction virtually. I received great feedback, and getting information from other teachers on how to teach virtually was the best form of professional development I could ever receive.

Giving Thanks **11/9/2020**

The grading period has begun, and here we go with another revised grading protocol from the district. This time, the grading protocol focused on "students' grades based upon grade-appropriate and standard-based assignments." We also had to encourage students to work through all school-wide and classroom interventions. The grading protocol comprises 45% of classwork and 35% of quizzes, tests, and projects. All formative and diagnostic assessments were 0%, which made sense since they were all questionable. However, since classwork was the highest percentage, I kept track of what the students completed and used my teacher's grade book to create an Excel sheet to send all parents what was missing and what was complete. Again, I kept plenty of documentation about students' grades and parent contact, just in case I had to fail a student, unfortunately.

This week, we also had our Fall costume Zoom party. This was cool because the counseling department used the book Tom Turkey to discuss social-emotional strategies and ways to cope with online learning. As a celebration, all students were to dress up as their favorite book characters. At 12:30 p.m., we logged into the counselor's Zoom call to listen to a story from the counselors. Afterward, we had an online dance party with the students' cameras on. This was a great way to break up our routine and celebrate the students, showing them that we can learn in various ways and that school can be fantastic even if we are virtual. This celebration was a true hit; I dressed up as Pete the Cat and danced virtually.

We were really in the spirit of giving thanks, and I had the students work on various giving thanks activities to discuss the importance of being grateful. We made turkeys using toilet paper rolls, paper, and glue, and during the week, we worked on a different turkey feather to write about what we were grateful for and why. I would tell the students to transfer that same information to ClassDojo and give a complete explanation of the topic of the day. We also used GetEpic to read different Thanksgiving books each day to learn about giving thanks and turkeys. This was an easy grade because they logged into their GetEpic accounts and took the required quizzes.

One thing I learned about virtual teaching is to keep all assignments as simple as possible. This makes it easier for the students to understand, and it encourages better participation.

Creative Thanksgiving **11/16/2020**

WE ARE SO CLOSE TO THANKSGIVING BREAK, AND I AM READY! This is the week before Thanksgiving, and I made my lessons as light as possible. One of the teachers at my school shared a Charlie Brown Thanksgiving Bitmoji Classroom that included a Charlie Brown Thanksgiving Book and activities focused on having a feast. This was a great lesson to teach for the week, and I was thankful to have it.

On day one, we listened to Charlie Brown's Thanksgiving story. The story was long, so I had to break it up into several days. After reading, the students would complete some comprehension questions on Dojo, and when they were done, they had free time to do a virtual Charlie Brown coloring page while listening to the Charlie Brown soundtrack.

On day two, we continued reading Charlie Brown's Thanksgiving, and I focused on vocabulary words such as feast. I told the students that we would have a Charlie Brown Feast on Friday, which included pretzels, popcorn, jellybeans, and a drink of choice. A list was sent to the parents so students were prepared for their feast, which we would have virtually.

Days three and four looked like one and two, and we continued to work on various reading comprehension activities and vocabulary words. The students' favorite activities were the virtual coloring pages and listening to the Charlie Brown Soundtrack. I noticed my students worked exceptionally hard so they could color as their reward. I might have to make this one of my incentives to get my work done! I tried one of the coloring pages myself, and I must admit it gave me a sense of relaxation and was a great brain break activity.

Friday was here, and we had the most fun! Students came on virtually; and the only thing they could focus on was, when we would have our feast! We started the virtual day recapping all the things we learned, and we went straight to our feast, which included popcorn, pretzels, jellybeans, drinks, and watched the Charlie Brown Thanksgiving movie. I had so many students participate in this activity, and some came up with their very own feast items they had at home. Seeing my students' excitement about the Charlie Brown Feast, Giving Thanks, and Thanksgiving made me feel good. This activity significantly impacted how they learned, and they became creative.

Happy Thanksgiving, Everyone!

CHAPTER EIGHT

HAPPY NEW YEAR 2021

New Year, Same Stuff **01/03/2021**

Our break is over, and we are returning to school with a modified schedule. It felt good to have a break from all the chaos and confusion of COVID-19. The fear and worry were driving my anxiety insane. But I knew we would eventually have to bite the bullet and return to work in the classroom, facing this virus head-on.

On January 3, teachers entered the building to set up and distribute devices to students who elected to remain virtual. With this new modified schedule, parents can choose to have their child stay virtual or return to school. There were numerous concerns regarding returning to the building, and to be honest, the district did not make it clear what our return would look like. We were told there would be an A Day and a B Day. This would include one set of students on Mondays and Wednesdays and another on Tuesdays and Thursdays, with Friday being virtual for all. We were also told that only 15 students would be on campus weekly, and the others would be virtual. We were all over the place, and nothing ever seemed clear.

We were finally informed that teachers could submit a hardship request to remain virtual for 30 days, from January 4 to February 4. During this period, teachers will work with the asynchronous remote schedule while preparing to return to the building after February 4. The teachers who do not complete the hardship application will begin working hybrid schedules on January 19th for Pre-K-2 and Jan 25th for grades 3–5. I had to decide. Will I complete the hardship form and remain remote until I am comfortable, or will I rip off the band-aid and dive in? This was so difficult; I was not only thinking about myself, but I also had a husband, children, and an elderly grandmother. However, I was tired of being at home and working from a computer, relying on food as my emotional support. I was bored at home and needed to find a new environment.

The time came, and I decided to take the plunge and dive in. The decision was difficult, but I knew I had to go back. Prolonging the situation would do nothing but cause me more anxiety. I would always be thinking about what if. There will always be the thought of how this would work. I knew the only way to make this work was to do it.

In preparation for our return, my principal sent emails seeking volunteers to help prepare the building for the students' return. To prepare, we put up signs stating the COVID rules, which include maintaining a six-foot distance when walking the halls, wearing masks daily, washing hands regularly, and cleaning up behind themselves, especially for students who switch classes. We placed floor decals in the hallway for students to line up with space between each other and on the walls. This took much of our time, but it was necessary for our safety.

Teachers were given upgraded computers with webcams, tripods, elmos, built-in microphones, and extended monitors. This would be valuable in supporting both remote and face-to-face teaching of students. I saw where schools were investing in high-tech technology such as motion-tracking webcams. I did not understand why some schools would invest more in some items than others. I wish the budget for COVID-19 was more detailed, outlining what the schools should spend their money on. We had an abundance of masks, gloves, cleaning supplies, and shields, which were needed, but the technology required just as much. One thing I learned about the pandemic is that there was no unison regarding education.

Hybrid Model **01/19/2021**

The week has come, and it is time to implement our instruction using the hybrid model. Hybrid means we will teach students both virtually and face-to-face. My roster consisted of approximately 22 students, with 12 attending face-to-face and 11 participating online. My schedule included meetings with students on Mondays, Tuesdays, Thursdays, and Fridays. Wednesdays were our designated work-from-home days.

When students entered the building, they went to the cafeteria, pick up their breakfast, and come to the classroom to eat. My desks were in rows, and I tried to have them six feet apart. Each student had a plastic shield on their desk and a water bottle holder on their chair. I gave my students their pencil pouches, including their pencils, crayons, glue sticks, and markers. I limited the use of books and notebooks since we used the hybrid model.

Instruction was challenging during this time. I had to learn how to keep up with both my remote students and my in-class students. The students who returned to the building were those who had not been actively remote during the shutdown. I was now trying to help these students acclimate to using their computers, logging in to the resources, and adjusting to returning to school after being at home and having their schedules. I dealt with students falling asleep in class and online, and let's not talk about students browsing other sites while instruction was taking place. I felt I had no control over my class, lessons, or anything else. Moreover, wearing a mask to teach made me feel as if I were suffocating, and when I took off the mask to wear a shield, my glasses would fog up. Everything was a mess, and the burnout and stress were REAL.

I wish we had two teachers in the class, one to implement face-to-face and the other to teach online. This would alleviate teachers' stress and pressure during this time. I felt as if I had to be two people at once, and there was not enough of me to go around. My students were very needy of my time and assistance. This was another primary concern once we returned to the classroom. I could tell the parents were doing most of the work, and the students were doing most of the watching.

Navigating through all this with the worry about COVID-19 and trying to get students to keep their masks on was overbearing. Our opening up was not thoroughly thought through. Some decisions look good on paper, but when they are implemented, they often become a different situation. This was only week one, and I was not in a good place.

Finding My Way **02/01/2021**

Several weeks later, the hybrid model is getting better, and I am finally adjusting to this new way of teaching. Upon arrival, I have my students do online work in the morning with their computers while I work with my face-to-face students. Instruction begins at 8 a.m., and I make all my students work online. I no longer juggle both. I converted my classroom into a remote online learning center, and all instruction was conducted on the computer. I worked behind my desk and stayed there the entire time. This was the best way for me to provide instruction and meet the needs of my online students and face-to-face kids. This also helps me avoid getting burned out and maintain my distance.

The district requests that all teachers return to the building by February 4th; no personal leave will be approved. I was relieved because I had already experienced all that the teachers coming back had to go through. We are also being asked to implement small group instruction and intervention in the morning. SMH!

Now that I finally feel like I've gotten my life together in the classroom, I have another task on my list of to-dos. One thing about education is that you will always have something to do, something new to learn, and something new to implement in instruction. It never ends!

Arrival time is used to support the implementation of small groups and targeted interventions. My class was still functioning as a remote learning center, and students were given a virtual schedule indicating which students I would meet with between 7:30 and 8:00 a.m. for the intervention block. I created a breakout room for this block for students to attend while I work on virtual instruction. This includes my face-to-face students as well. Again, I maintained my social distance and was able to meet the needs of all. Small groups also looked like my intervention block. The small group block was held in the afternoon after recess. Students were given independent work, whether face-to-face or online, and I would meet with my specific small group of students in a breakout room I created on Teams. This was the only way I knew how to meet my students' needs and the district's demands. This also worked well with my ESOL teacher, who was now working using the hybrid model. We were able to collaborate and work cohesively to ensure that her students received ESOL instruction while my students received small group reading instruction.

Tornado Drill **2/15/2021**

No school on Monday! Thank God for this day off! I need a day to breathe and not think about hybrid learning, social distancing, COVID-19, or anything else about work. The burnout was real, and I was exhausted! I took this day to work out, meditate, spend time with family, and breathe!

I'm back to reality with an email that has something new to do. This week, we had focus walks on our guided reading instruction and a tornado drill. I am trying to figure out why we are doing focus walks in a non-traditional teaching setting. Focus walks consist of a group of administrators, coaches, and, at times, district representatives who come around to observe your instruction. This walk focused on how we conduct reading instruction using the provided resources in a hybrid setting. During this time, teachers will receive feedback on what was observed using the grows and glows model. Several teachers were selected, but not all of them, and I was chosen for this focus walk. WHYYYYYYY!?!?!?!

It was focus walk day, and I was prepared to teach my class precisely the way I had taught the other day. The only difference is that I used my co-teacher's mobile desk cart and implemented my instruction in front of my board instead of behind my desk. During the focus walk, my instruction for the day targeted the reading strategy of beginning, middle, and end. I read the day's story aloud to my students, both online and in person. I downloaded a graphic organizer with a beginning, middle, and end as its focal point, and our whole-group instruction focused on completing the graphic organizer virtually. As an independent lesson, I assigned a story to my students using GetEpic and had them complete the same graphic organizer we previously worked on in whole-group instruction. The exit ticket was to share what they wrote. The lesson went well, and I got many glows. The only growth I was given was to be more interactive with my face-to-face students. Good feedback, but I was still maintaining social distancing. This was not a traditional teaching setting, nor were we in a conventional situation. I was going to support my six feet, which was necessary.

The week was almost over, but we had something else on the schedule!!! TORNADO DRILL! Smh! Our tornado drill was scheduled for 9 a.m., and we had to notify our online students that a tornado drill was taking place at school and ask them to remain in place until it was over. Our face-to-face students had to get up and go into the hallway to lie face down in the hall until the drill was over. Once the drill was over, we returned to class to continue our instruction. I checked in on my online students and realized that many of them had left. They thought the drill meant school was over, and of course, when I tried to call them back into class, I received no answer. Oh well, this is the life of a teacher teaching during the pandemic!

Black History Week **2/22/2021**

We are having a PTA/Black History program and a cultural awareness program in the last week of February. All of this was going to be online. I wanted to see how this would work and hoped it would be nice. The way it was planned out was exciting to see, and students were looking forward to attending, especially those participating.

It's event day, and at 1 p.m., students were to log in to Teams using the school link to view our schoolwide Black History program. This turned out to be nice. Students who came to school face-to-face were the ones performing. The school link allowed us to see the students performing on stage in the cafeteria. Teachers served as tech support and helped mute students who were entering the channel or simply pressed the mute button. It was great to see students celebrating Black History and being active in school during these unprecedented times. The program lasted an hour, and then it was time for dismissal. Students were encouraged to log back into our schoolwide Teams link for our PTA meeting and cultural awareness event.

It is 5 p.m., and I am currently online working overtime for our PTA cultural event. This event was a little more interesting and chaotic. First, many students had logged in, and there was no way to control the mute button. For the Black History event, most students logged in to their teacher's site, and the teacher logged into the school site. It made it easier for technology control. This, on the other hand, was way different. Then, there were no clear directives for cultural awareness on how this event was supposed to go. It was turning on your screens to show your cultural outfit. So many screens were on, so many students were talking simultaneously, and you did not know who you were looking at or what you were looking at. My principal and several teachers were yelling one at a time on the screen, but students weren't listening, and it was all over the place. I understood what we were trying to do, but I don't think actual planning was done to ensure this event went smoothly. But hey, nothing goes well when the computer is your primary source of instruction. This was one of those situations in which you live and learn. I'm glad it's over because we still have two more days to work this week. GEESH!

During the pandemic, teachers worked more overtime than ever. The job never felt like it ended. We would go home, but then there were online meetings or programs in the afternoons. We also had to plan and grade papers. I was always working, and on top of that, I was also working as a tutor to help fill some of the gaps, which could have been the source of this overworked feeling. But no matter what, teachers worked the hardest during this tumultuous time.

CHAPTER NINE

READ ACROSS AMERICA VIRTUALLY

Cohorts, Geesh **03/01/2021**

It was a rainy morning and another change; this time, many more parents were asking students to return to school. Many jobs now require parents to return, and, above all, parents are exhausted with virtual learning. So, what does this mean? We must now implement the days for Cohort A and Cohort B. This allows us to increase the number of students returning to the classroom. We were now asked to label our desks with either A or B labels. This will inform students of their assigned seating when they arrive at school. We had to have mandated sanitation stations along with desks six feet apart. A school-wide roster was created to identify which students had siblings in other grades, allowing them to be placed on the same cohort day. This required a lot of work and meticulous planning. This also means an end to remote learning. We were slowly transitioning back to normal, but not every day. It was a way to get students back into the building and work towards what it used to be.

Not only were we now implementing these chart days, but we also had Read Across America Week, during which we celebrated Dr. Seuss and the joy of reading. We focused on the return to school as a fun experience by having students dress up in a different Dr. Seuss theme. Monday was our Fox in Socks Day. Students could come to school in cool socks to show off to their peers. Tuesday was Cat in the Hat Day. Students came to school wearing their hats. Wednesday was a Wacky Day. Dress in your best wacky wear. Thursday was Green Eggs and Ham Day: Wear your best green outfit. On Friday, we wrapped it up with 'Oh the Places You'll Go'; this day was the day students dressed up for their future careers.

With the Cohort Days, A Days were in person while B Day students worked independently at home, and vice versa. As a teacher, instruction was repeated. What you taught for A, you had to reteach for B. Of course, I had a hard time keeping up at first. I had to write everything down on what I taught A to remember what I needed to teach B. I had to recreate my small groups because students were split up, and my interventions were almost nonexistent because I was trying to keep up with this new change. Students will arrive at 7:15 a.m. with breakfast; I had to ensure that my desks were six feet apart, but now it was more difficult because of the increase in the number of students coming in on both days. A Day had more students due to the number of siblings in the school. I went from 12 to 14 on days A and B. Parents were also confused. Students who were supposed to come on A Day would come on B Day, and so forth. We were not allowed to turn any students away, even if they arrived on the wrong day. It was a struggle; again, I felt all over the place.

There were days when I would go home and not eat but go to bed instead. The feeling of being overwhelmed and anxious was getting the best of me. There were too many changes within a short period, and I never felt I could adjust to this new way of doing things. At this point, I am only thinking about summer break because this is becoming too much.

Literacy Night **03/08/2021**

Literacy night is this week. Is the district now changing all students' passwords? Yes, another change is underway. I'm telling you; it's never a dull moment in the world of education. This week, students will learn a new method for logging in to the computer for security reasons. Students must now learn how to log in using their student ID number, birthdate, and asterisk. This is not just for upper grades, but for all grade levels. That means a kindergarten student must know how to enter the password s933333Sep16$. Unbelievable!!! This would occur the week we have literacy night; our new schedule was implemented last week. Students will now use this as their password while attending any school in the county. As if we didn't have enough on our plates, here's another lesson that needs to be taught. Every morning during intervention time, I worked with my students logging in using their new passwords. We also used fake paper keyboards to practice how students should place their hands while typing in their information. This was a great way to help my students increase their typing confidence and understand how to use the keyboard effectively. During the pandemic, students were forced to learn how to type but did not understand the fundamentals of the keyboard.

While all this was happening, ESOL students were also working on access testing. This is when ESOL teachers assess students to determine if they have demonstrated any growth in the ESOL program. Instruction this time focused on review. I had a class of 14 ESOL students, which means many of my students were pulled for testing this week. I had worked on closing the learning gaps through targeted interventions and small-group instruction.

Literacy night is also this week, and that went well. Each grade level had its link, and each presented something different regarding literacy night. My first-grade team read a book by Dr. Seuss, and we worked on the digital activities created by Dr. Seuss. We had a great deal of fun, and the students were fully engaged. This program was way better than the last, and it was easier for us to break it up into breakout sessions than using a single schoolwide link.

Overall, this week was not that bad, with low numbers due to testing and the focus on learning to log in. Instruction this week was straightforward, and from the looks of things, it will remain simple from now on. Testing starts, including MAP, Milestones, Access, and Benchmarks.

Teacher Duties **03/16/2021**

Professional development week and no school for students. A mandatory email was sent to all teachers, giving instructions on our new professional development for the remainder of the year. We will meet virtually by signing up for the professional development (PD) that meets your criteria. All large-group professional development sessions were canceled, and teachers had to use that time to work in their classrooms. This was a good time to catch up on much-needed sanitation, grades, and parent contact logs. I used this time to focus on what I wanted to teach my students for the remainder of the year. There was so much to learn and so little time. I also had to consider all the mandated testing that impacts instruction. I did not understand why we were testing these kids. It does not make sense to test them when we already know they have lost so many foundational skills, and we were not teaching these kids in the same way. What fundamental data can you get to tell you the truth? They won't do well due to the impact on instruction and all the changes we've gone through this year. Education never makes sense. I would love to speak with whoever develops these recommendations. They never worked in the classroom before.

When the students returned to the classroom, we were testing for benchmarks. If you are familiar with benchmarks, this test serves as a formative assessment that demonstrates what students have learned from the previous unit across all subjects. Just like I thought, my students did terribly. SMH! I hate taking benchmarks in my district. The test is complicated, and the language is too advanced for my English as a Second Language (ESOL) students. Not only that, but our instruction pacing was not aligned with the benchmarks, so some of the learning targets on the test were not covered in class. It's senseless. But if this is what they want, I will follow the rules and pray that one day these students would not be subjected to a test score and given actual instruction that focuses on real-world events and moves forward with all the changes we see in technology and careers. Students need classes focusing on financial literacy, STEM, computer courses, reading, writing, life skills, and physical education. That is what we should be teaching these kids today. This is what is needed because this is what they lack.

I woke up on the morning of the 18th with a news report stating lousy weather in Atlanta! It was an inclement weather day and a day off!!! YESSS! God knew exactly what I needed during this time, and I was genuinely thankful.

Dojo and Glowsticks Party 3/22/2021

Last week had its ups and downs. Hopefully, this week will be more consistent. Due to inclement weather, we have scheduled makeup tests for the benchmarks. We also have our student of the month celebrations and a glow stick party. The Student of the Month celebrations highlight students who embody the month's core values. These students can have waffles with our principal and engage with other students from other grades. Students work hard to be part of the Student of the Month celebration. They also enjoy seeing their pictures displayed in the hallway with a note from their teacher. I appreciate that the Student of the Month has an intimate setting where they can engage with our principal.

The glow stick party is an overall school-wide discipline initiative. Students who display our school rules in and out of the classroom are eligible to purchase glow sticks and celebrate during lunch. Students love this because they watch as our principal is the school DJ, wearing glowsticks, and the students dance to the latest kid-friendly songs while having lunch with their peers. It's charming, and the students again work hard to be part of this fabulous event. I also like it because I use it as a discipline tool throughout the month, along with the Dojo points. In my class, students who do not have 30 or more points for that month are not eligible to attend the glow stick party. My students do not play around with their Dojo points; they work hard to earn those 30 points. It's really a win-win in classroom management.

This week, we also have a celebratory staff meeting. In this meeting, we gather in the cafeteria to celebrate the Employee of the Month and the birthdays of the month. We sing for those teachers and celebrate the newly elected employee of the month. As employee of the month, you get a trophy, a gift card, and a parking space in front of the school. It's a way for teachers to feel valued and know that their hard work is not in vain.

March Madness **03/29/2021**

This week is virtual March Madness for upper grades, and it's our last week until spring break. We are looking forward to the break, and I need peace and rest. This week in class, we will work on new content to prepare for any makeup testing and the final week of Access assessments.

Students also worked on missing assignments this week while I met with my small groups and interventions. This was a good opportunity for students to catch up on their grades, which were approaching quickly. With this new way of teaching, we had to provide ample time for students to make up for missing work and give any extra assignments to prevent failing. You can tell which students took advantage of this and which didn't have the resources or support. The pandemic revealed a great deal about the state of education. Many teachers found themselves in a position where they were unable to return to the profession due to a lack of support and an extensive workload. There were also complaints about pay. We deserve way more than what we are getting, and what baffles me is that we are the backbone of so many careers. Without educators, you won't have doctors, lawyers, firefighters, actors, or basketball players. So, why are we paid so little?

Our librarian hosted a pop-up shop this week to encourage reading during spring break, and students visited the library to check out books. These books were used for students to read, and they could use a reading log to win a free small pizza coupon. I noticed that students needed more encouragement than ever to read and stay on task. The good part about technology is that it gives students access to learning a great deal, but the bad part is that it can be a massive distraction, making it difficult for students to stay focused and motivated to learn. Teachers were now battling teaching and technology, keeping students engaged and focused. Teaching now had to be creative, relatable, and technology driven.

CHAPTER TEN

CLOSING OUT 2021

Countdown to Summer **04/12/2021**

After spring break, I had a wonderful time relaxing and spending quality time with my family. I took advantage of the week and just stopped! It was time to disconnect from technology and reconnect with nature. I learned during this pandemic that I needed to get closer to GOD and my ancestors. I needed direction and guidance. This world can be complicated, and with the stress of work, I needed a higher power to help me get through my daily life.

As we began our countdown to the end of the school year, upper grades focused on Milestones, while lower grades concentrated on MAP and preparations for the next school year. In first grade, we began creating lesson plans as if we were in second grade and teaching the beginning of second-grade standards. We met with the second-grade teachers during our collaborative planning session to gain an understanding of what we needed to focus on as our learning target for the remainder of the year. Even though many of my students demonstrated learning gaps, we continued to implement complex instruction to enhance students' vocabulary and comprehension. Introducing complex texts helps students to analyze and evaluate information, learn how to problem-solve, and navigate through challenging assignments while exploring diverse viewpoints.

April is a month that tends to pass quickly due to the last-minute demands from administrators and instructors. We also wanted to become a STEAM school. This was the month when we intentionally created STEAM-related lessons. Students also went to STEM classes to develop an understanding of natural phenomena, the scientific method, and inquiry-based learning. Basics of computer science (coding, programming, app development), digital tools (e.g., 3D printing, simulations, software applications), familiarity with modern technological innovations and how they shape industries, engineering design principles: planning, prototyping, and testing, problem-solving through systems thinking and structural logic and applications in fields like robotics, environmental design, and aerospace. Some of the activities students worked on were building using toothpicks and creating towers out of paper towel rolls. Students love STEM and having the opportunity to develop. I appreciate how students utilized their creative talents in areas beyond the computer.

This week, we returned to continue our learning using our pacing guide. Teachers are given a pacing guide at the beginning of the school year to show where they should be in their instruction throughout the school year. This has been a unique school year, so our pacing guide has been revised several times. A pacing guide is necessary to get to all the standards we should teach for that specific grade. I used this week to continue our pacing and review learning targets for students who may have breezed through them. After spring break, students and teachers are refreshed, and teaching becomes more straightforward; however, we are also in a spring mindset at the end of the school year. This is when we students tend to get most distracted, and teachers are just ready for the year to end.

Earth Day and MAP **04/19/2021**

It's Earth Day week, and we are big on celebrating Earth Day. This week, we worked on STEM activities that helped the earth, discussed the three Rs (reduce, reuse, and recycle), and demonstrated hands-on Earth Day activities throughout the building. One of the activities we did in first grade was to use alligator claws and pick up paper outside on the playground. We also discussed not touching anything you do not notice or that looks unsafe. Ask a teacher first before picking it up! We grew plants around our school (we had a garden on the side of the building), and students from Georgia State came in to discuss the importance of developing food and caring for crops. Students also took some crops home to make an excellent dish with their families. Celebrating Earth Day is a lot of fun, and I wish it lasted longer than just a week. I wish there were a way to incorporate more Earth Day activities throughout the school year.

While celebrating Earth Day, we were preparing for our Map assessment, which was scheduled for April 26, and benchmarks online on May 3. Since we had more time with benchmarks, we utilized resources such as MAP Skills Navigator, MobyMax, Raz-Kids, and Teachers Pay Teachers to help teach students the specific domains assessed by the MAP. I like the MAP test, but I do not want the pressure. MAP is an adaptive test and shows students' growth based on what was taught throughout the school term. In the spring, students are to show a certain level of development. This test is a valuable resource to help teachers determine what to teach and how to support their students. But at my school, it feels more like competition. Teachers are awarded certificates and shoutouts in our meetings to meet their MAP goals. Teachers even gave big prizes to students when they met their MAP goals. Yes, we need data, but to what extent? Are we supposed to put this much pressure on students and teachers to meet a testing goal when the test is created to help teachers know what to teach their students? Testing has become too much of a focal point in education, and students feel pressured to do so. It's not good for them. I think when we put this much pressure on students to meet a testing goal, we are creating anxiety, depression, competition, and divisiveness. Testing can be fun, but it is also too stressful, and as I have learned after COVID-19, it has only gotten worse.

Reading Deficiencies **04/26/2021**

It's the second week of Milestone for upper grades and MAP testing for lower grades. Since we are administering the MAP assessment, students take it in the morning and review it in the afternoon. We also worked on small group instruction and interventions.

This was also the week we had our first vertical alignment sessions. These are collaborative sessions between teachers, led by teachers or grade-level chairs, such as weekly grade-level meetings. Links were provided, and a presentation was provided to guide you through the discussion points. The admin will circulate from meeting to meeting to hear us discuss specific focal points. In our meeting, the first-grade teachers planned to discuss upcoming lessons, resources, assessments, and ways to collaborate on teaching these subjects. We also discussed ways to close the gaps by using spiral review sheets to meet all standards in one setting and using RAZ Kids phonics to hit those key phonetic skills. We have learned that many of our students were struggling with reading and having difficulty with phonetics and decoding. This was not an easy task to teach when we were in the middle of a pandemic and had to wear a mask. To teach decoding strategies, students need to see mouth placement, and during a pandemic, reading requires intense instruction. Truthfully, there was never enough time to prepare it all. I wish we had two teachers during this time to help meet all the demands we were facing.

COVID has caused a reading deficiency in many ways due to the interruption in instruction and the changes. Many of my students were reading at a kindergarten level or not knowing how to read at all. How would this look two to three years from now, and what steps will we take to support these students? This is scary, and the students are failing miserably. The pandemic catalyzed rapid innovation and highlighted systemic educational inequalities, resulting in long-term shifts in education delivery and student retention.

Teacher Appreciation **05/03/2021**

OOOOH May! What a joy to see! It is Teacher Appreciation Week! This week, so much love was shown. Our administration provided us with T-shirts, masks, fanny packs, lunch, breakfast, and snacks. Students also made us cards, gave us flowers, sent gift cards to our favorite restaurants, and did many other thoughtful things. It feels good to be appreciated because this job isn't easy.

This week, students were assessed using benchmarks, our unit assessments. The benchmarks can be challenging for our students, especially our ESOL population, who struggle with vocabulary and comprehension. This assessment determines how much students have learned at the end of the unit, and my students did not do well. They are going to need a lot of intervention next year.

This week, we also gave out report cards online, which were new to parents, but I liked it a lot. It eliminated a significant amount of paper and was an excellent resource for parents to track their child's grades on Infinite Campus. They no longer had to depend on the teacher. They can now use online resources to track grades and attendance.

We had four weeks left in school, and there was a significant push to ensure that our small groups were still being implemented and receiving targeted intervention. The first-grade team provided second-grade standard instruction and reviewed it over the past four weeks. We wanted to expose our students to what they would experience in second grade, but we made a concerted effort to close any learning gaps first. Even though this was a difficult task, consistency was key, and we hoped that what we taught would stick.

This week, we also had a field day with our students. The field day was an event where students competed against other classes in PE-related skills. Field day is big at my school! We have the KONA ice truck, and the school is divided into different sections so that students can participate in activities such as a one-legged race, tug-of-war, ring toss, egg race, relay, and many more. This was when students could let their hair down, run, share with their friends, and be kids. The teachers would get involved, too, racing each other and encouraging their students to do their best and WIN! Field day is a joy; administrators, teachers, students, and parents love it!

Blossoming May **05/10/2021**

May is fun and exciting, but it is also hectic! We celebrated our school nurse for Nurse Appreciation Day, our awards day this week, and Career Day. GEESH!! Instruction was primarily small group and review setting, but with all these activities, it was challenging to implement anything throughout the day.

First grade awards day was on Tuesday of this week, and everything had to be done online due to the pandemic. Parents logged in around 9 a.m. on our first-grade link, and each teacher presented their awards. We had our cameras on, and as a screensaver, one of the first-grade teachers created a Bitmoji representing the teacher presenting their awards. This made the presentation interactive and fun. Awards day was very different this year due to the pandemic, but it was also successful, and students felt appreciated. In the past, our awards day was held in the cafeteria, where parents could enter the building to watch their child walk across the stage to receive their certificate and medals if they were on the principal's list, honor roll, or Mustang Student of the Year.

Career Day was also a huge success this year, and of course, this looked different as well. Our Career Day was held on Friday, and we had a variety of presenters who joined us via our team link to talk to us about their careers. Firefighters arrived at our school to talk about their job; a storyteller read a book to us online, and we also had a visit from a baker and a mailman. We were also given activity packets when a presenter did not show up for students to work during that specific time. Career Day was fun and informative, and the kids enjoyed it! Kudos to our counselors for a successful Career Day!

Although we had numerous great activities, we also had to attend our weekly meetings. I'm telling you, it never stops! This week's vertical planning involves first-grade teachers meeting with second-grade teachers to discuss expectations, standards, and areas for improvement as a first-grade team, based on the second-grade team's observations. The second-grade students gave us a lot of positive feedback and told us they saw our hard work. Our students come in ready to learn and are prepared. It felt good to hear our hard work wasn't in vain. After speaking with the second-grade team, our next session was to collaborate with the kindergarten teachers to discuss how they can prepare their students for first grade. Kinder also does a great job preparing their students for first. The only thing we would like to see our kinders focus more on is independence.

Our last meeting, which was optional, was a meeting one of our first-grade teachers came up with, called Swap Meet. This meeting took place after school on Teams, where teachers would share ideas. This Swap Meeting focused on the differences between old-school teachers and new-school teachers. I was a presenter and presented ways to facilitate small groups using RAZ-KIDS. With over 20 years of experience, I was known as an old-school teacher. At the same time, the new school teacher demonstrated how she utilized various technology resources, including whiteboards, QR codes, and a toy theater, for interactive math manipulatives.

Are We Done Yet? **05/17/2021**

NOPE! One more week and summer break, here we come! This week, students were required to turn in their devices to the media center, and we used work packets as our primary form of instruction. This week, teachers completed their end-of-the-year grades and started breaking down their classes.

We had our first annual schoolwide movie day, where the entire school watched G-rated movies, ate popcorn provided by the administration, and students came in wearing their pajamas. On this day, teachers moved all desks to the back of the room, and students sat on blankets or towels from home to enjoy their movies. I used this day to finalize inputting my grades, ensure all my RTI information was up to date, and complete my end-of-the-year checklist provided by my AP. Yes, it was a lot to do, but it was also time to bid farewell to the old and prepare for the new.

As sad as I am to see my students go, I am grateful to see this year come to an end. This was a challenging school term for us all, marked by numerous challenges, changes, and learning curves. This school year tested my teaching abilities and my effectiveness as a teacher. I had to grow in ways I never knew before. Collaboration was key to helping us get through the tough times. Learning about all the different types of technology devices and resources was new but necessary. I'm not sure what the future holds, but education will never look the same again!

Goodbye 2022 **05/24/2021**

The end is here; it is finally time to say goodbye to my students. It is so sad to see them go, but this is when they need to grow. My students faced many challenges this year, but are resilient and tech-savvy. They are kids who love learning, and I know they will continue to blossom through the years.

I look forward to seeing what they accomplish in three to four years and the strengths they have developed from the pandemic.

I am grateful to have worked with a team of teachers who could navigate all the craziness while still focusing on providing students with meaningful instruction. We worked together and fought one of the most brutal battles we would ever have to face in our teaching journey.

I am thankful to have worked at a school where everyone came together to provide the best for the students. We showed up and showed out. There were times when we didn't know how we were going to do it, but we managed to do it. One thing I appreciate about my school is that the teachers there are like family, and we laugh together, cry on each other's shoulders, and offer ultimate support. We are each other's cheerleaders and want to see each other win! I love that about my school, and I am grateful to be in a community filled with so much love and togetherness.

I am happy to say we have parents who cherish what we do and how we teach their children. They look to us as role models and for guidance. They come to us with their deepest concerns and show us gratitude. Our parents are the best, and they show it in their support and actions.

Lastly, as we reflect on this school year, it is impossible not to acknowledge the extraordinary challenges we all faced during the COVID-19 pandemic, particularly in the education sector. I thank the administration for their unwavering dedication and resilience throughout this unprecedented time.

Your leadership and determination ensured that students, parents, and staff alike continued to have access to learning, connection, and support despite overwhelming obstacles. Navigating constantly shifting health guidelines, overcoming technological barriers, and prioritizing the well-being of our community were not just administrative tasks; they were acts of compassion and courage.

The countless hours you spent organizing virtual classes, ensuring resources reached those in need, and making difficult decisions did not go unnoticed. Your creativity and adaptability in implementing hybrid models, addressing access gaps, and fostering a sense of normalcy amidst chaos were remarkable.

I am profoundly grateful for these efforts—and for so much more. Your commitment was a beacon of hope when our students, families, and faculty needed it most. You have not just managed through a crisis; you have built a legacy of perseverance and care that will inspire us all for years to come.

To my school family, thank you for leading with empathy, integrity, and an unyielding belief in the power of education. Your contributions have made an indelible mark on this community, and we are better because of our dedication.

Call to Action: Helping Students Thrive After the Pandemic

As highlighted in *Teaching During the Pandemic*, the learning gaps left in the wake of COVID-19 are real—and they require intentional, compassionate, and strategic efforts to close. That's why I created **Sessom Masterminds**, a tutoring service dedicated to helping students in grades K–5 regain their confidence and rebuild essential academic skills.

Our Focus Areas Include:

- **Reading & Phonetics**
- **Writing & Grammar**
- **Math Fundamentals**
- **Comprehension Strategies**

Sessom Masterminds offers **one-on-one tutoring sessions** that are engaging, tech-savvy, and tailored to each child's unique needs. Our goal is to not only support academic success, but to spark creativity and curiosity in learning, especially for students who fell behind during remote instruction.

This isn't just tutoring, it's a mission to get students back on track, restore their love for learning, and prepare them for a successful future.

SESSOM MASTERMINDS
Tutorial Services
READING
TUTORIAL
PROGRAM
FOR K-5TH GRADERS
MOTIVATIONS
SCAN QR CODE
ESOL CERTIFIED
GIFTED CERTIFIED
BIRTH-K CERTIFIED
EDS IN EDUCATION
P-5 CERTIFIED
20+ Years Teaching Experience
Program Include:
• one on one services
• must be able to transport student to my tutorial location
• must commit to two hour minimum
913-303-1449
Contact me now to secure your child's spot

About the Author

Professional Summary:

Dawn Sessom is a dedicated and passionate elementary educator with over 20 years of experience shaping young minds and fostering a love for learning. Her innovative teaching methods and a deep understanding of child development have consistently resulted in exceptional student outcomes and a nurturing classroom environment.

Educational Background:

- Bachelor of Arts in Elementary Education, Clark Atlanta University (2000)
- Master of Science in Adult Education, Adult Education (2015)
- Master of Arts in Teaching, Mercer University (2019)
- Education Specialist, Walden University (2017)

Professional Experience:

- Charles R Drew Charter School, Atlanta, GA- Kindergarten
- YMCA Lithonia- Pre-K
- Hamilton Headstart- Pre-K
- Clifton School, Atlanta- Pre-K

- Indian Creek Elementary- first grade
- Present Employment
- Idlewood Elementary- 1st and 3rd

Performance:

Successfully led school-wide initiatives to improve literacy, resulting in a 50% increase in reading proficiency over five years based on MAP data.

Conduct PD training on Guided Reading and using various technology resources.

Teaching Philosophy:

Dawn believes that every child has unique strengths and potential. Her teaching philosophy centers on creating a supportive and inclusive classroom where students feel valued and inspired to learn. She emphasizes fostering critical thinking, creativity, and a lifelong love for learning.

Personal Interests:

Dawn enjoys being a wife to Edward Sessom and a mother to Amari, Tyler, Jordan, Kyndall, and Trey. I love eating at different restaurants, being with close friends, exercising with my crew and awesome personal trainer, traveling, and shopping. Gardening and getting facials are the ultimate self-care!

Dawn's two decades of dedication to elementary education demonstrate her unwavering commitment to positively impacting her students' lives and her continuous pursuit of excellence in teaching.

Facebook: https://www.facebook.com/dawn.miles.75
Instagram: https://www.instagram.com/luvnme4ever